STAY IN THE BOAT DEVOTIONAL BOOK

30 DAYS OF HOPE FOR HARD TIMES

VALERIE DAVIS BENTON   VICTORIA RUTH DAVIS

ANDREA DOZIER   BETHANY KIMSEY

CANDACE ROBERTS   SUSAN SANDERS   A. T. WARI

Red Ink Circle

Some aspects of this book are memoir. It reflects the authors' present recollections of experiences over time. Some names and characteristics have been changed, some events may have been compressed, and some dialogue has been recreated. We have shared all stories to the best of our recollection.

 Created with Vellum

CONTENTS

May this book and all we say
honor You, Lord, until The Day,
but above all, we praise the
Author and Finisher of our faith.

We ink a special note of love and dedication to Pastor Michael Catt
from the authors of this book who call you our pastor, friend, and
mentor. Your legacy will live long upon the earth until we all meet
again in the glory of God's presence. We also ink a note of love and
dedication to Terri Catt, a leader of women with a heart of gold.

We also note our thanks to all the Christian female — and male —
authors who have gone before us and set the bar for us when using
our pens as literary missionaries.

WHY STAY IN THE BOAT?

INTRODUCTION

VICTORIA RUTH DAVIS WITH CANDACE ROBERTS

The little one-person ducky-canoe shoots through the eddies, quiet waters, and fierce rapids of the Nantahala River, propelled by my double-sided paddle. Well, these rapids *fiercely tumble* in my opinion, anyway.

Even on this brisk summer day in July 2020, when the pandemic painted the people off this usually crowded river into an empty canvas upon which we can brush the strokes of adventure, these waters can deliver both joy — and danger.

Although we've paddled this river dozens of times — usually in these solo duckies (rafts) where you truly "row your own boat" or face the rocky consequences — we always follow a trained guide who knows the path better than we do.

I'm sure from the shore it looks like I'm happily splashing and sliding easily through the maze of jagged rocks. However, bystanders are clueless about the rocky jabs coming through the thin boat bottom or the thick fear that overwhelms me as I play catch up with our guide and prepare for what's ahead.

I know that this trip climaxes at the Nantahala Falls or "Little Wesser," as it was called back when I began traversing this river in the 1970s. We always hop out of our rafts and walk ahead to scout these falls since they pose realistic danger.

Several years ago, too many family members tried to "shoot the falls" without proper distancing. As a result, two of our party fell out of their boats and had "life *splashing* before your eyes" experiences. This event we now call "ducky carnage," resulted in several of our group refusing to brave this rapid again. But not me.

WILL I FACE MY FEAR?

Today, and always, I must feel the fear *and* make a decision. Will I abandon my boat and walk around, or will I stay in the boat and face the falls?

Down I go. I must face this … along with everything else I've experienced so far in 2020. From running my first half-marathon at 50, to my husband's job change, to Mom's dementia, to my youngest child graduating from high school and another from college, to the relentless cascade of tasks required to manage distance learning for my school, this year has brought rapids that must be faced head-on, regardless of the fear and anxiety they bring.

So I grip my paddle and head for the falls.

WHICH WAY WILL I GO?

Three possible routes through the rapids are navigable. Guides call these "lines" and like the roads on a map, they can take you down safely. Unlike roads on a map, they have no edge and there are really millions of ways down a rapid. For this rapid, there are three lines:

A-line hugs the right side and is a nice ride, except for the rocky ledge at the bottom. This ledge tips most duckies over, sending the rafter swimming.

Most ducky rafters aim for the *B-line* for safety. However, it runs just to the right of the boat-sucking vortex of under-current in the middle of the rapid. Because of a slight veer to the right, this is where two family members had their boats sucked out from under them, experiencing a terrifying washing machine cycle while being spun like laundry and tossed out when the river felt like it. But, if you hit *B-line* the right way and paddle hard, "yahoo," can't even begin to express the fun it would be.

Larger rafts prefer *C-line* which is to the left of B, but it isn't so suitable for our tiny duckies.

However, I've seen duckies go down all three lines successfully. The secret is forward momentum. When you paddle hard, never stop, and press forward no matter what — you can make it through most anything. Kind of like life. Once you commit, go full steam ahead. The only real danger is if you stop paddling altogether or overtake another rafter who hasn't finished their run. Mid rapid is never a time to hesitate!

TAKING ON THE FALLS

So this time, while I aim for B-line, the river has other plans. I navigate slightly too far right, shooting me down A-line. The drop brings a "whoosh" of breath through my lips. I know I will make it down the falls, but I'm bracing for the shoals that threaten to tip me at the bottom.

As I paddle through, I look downriver for the ledge and don't see the rock right in front of me that starts me spinning. What a mess! I'm heading onto the rapids sideways and backwards as the photographer is using her high-speed sports photography to capture my demise. She lives on this river and she thinks I'm going in!

No! I pray as I use every bit of leverage, lean, and fight in me to counterbalance my boat and keep it upright. It is precariously tipping past the point of no return. Everything that has happened in 2020 flows in on me in this moment.

STAY IN THE BOAT

I've made it down the whole river. My deep desire is to finish and stay in the boat.

Sheryl Sandburg, COO of Facebook, says "lean in," but sometimes you've gotta lean away! Leaning down into the part of the boat being tipped over the falls would mean I was going in and I didn't want that. Even though my wet suit would keep me from being too cold — nothing, and I mean nothing, can prevent the bruises and gashes of sharp rocks.

You see, on a river, it usually isn't the visible stuff that hurts you — it is the jagged unknown stuff underneath the surface that entraps and injures you. Never think because you can't see it that no danger exists.

So, with everything I have, I lean away and work to stabilize my boat. I finally clear the rapids and paddle exhaustedly to the shore and finish the trip with a big smile.

FIGHTING THE TIPPING POINT

Leroy Eims in his book *Be the Leader You Were Meant to Be* says leaders make an impact with wholeheartedness, single-mindedness, and a fighting spirit. As I reflect upon this moment as I fought the impact of going in, I'm reminded of Eim's assertion.

I pray down the whole river! Then, as I single-mindedly fought with my whole heart, God gave me the fighting spirit to finish well. Everything in me knew I could slightly lean towards the water and end the fight. I'd be in, but that wouldn't make anything better — not in the pandemic and not on this short river trip!

Stay in the boat! When things are tough, it is easy to just want change. Anywhere else, anybody else, just take me away from this! "Get me outta here!" we cry to God in the night.

But we forget that unseen dangers and rapid changes fill the river of life, no matter which line of life we take. We need a guide. We need momentum. We need lots of prayer. A fighting spirit.

Just look how rapidly a global lockdown rolled over the world like a waterfall off a cliff.

In our 2020 experience and since my July trip down the river, every surprise eddy and turn has had me pondering how easy it is to tip over — mentally, physically, and perhaps even spiritually.

Sickness. Funerals. Fever. Goodbyes. Politics. Surgery. Pain. Suffering. Sadness. There have been times it has been tempting, for sure, to give in to the lean and just let myself fall out.

I can go under, retreat, and let myself float downstream boatless, as one with the river of life. Every commitment, every plan, every moment: just gone. Out of the boat. I can close my door, refuse to boot up my computer, and find an escape of choice to forget about where I am.

I think if we are honest, we'll admit many of us have tipped precipitously these days. Many are on the edge of danger, tipping towards an unhealthy and unholy place of self-pity and panic. Perhaps that's where you are now.

WHAT WE WANT FOR YOU

The pictures from the photographer, who captured my 2020 adventure at the Falls, show it as a smooth experience over several minutes, but in reality, my desperate fight with the water only lasted seconds.

I showed my friends in the Red Ink Circle these pictures several weeks after my trip, and we howled in laughter at my battle to stay in the boat.

Then later, as we discussed what we wanted to share in this book of devotionals, Andrea laughed in that infectious way she does and said,

 "Vicki, staying in that boat. I think that is what we want people to do. We want them to stay in the boat."

We all share our own stories — many are in these pages. We want to encourage people to live their lives and move forward through life with purpose and joy.

WE WANT YOU TO SUCCEED

Whether you've fallen in or think you're going under — cry out! Jesus awaits you on the shore with a rope. He will pull you out and save you.

Your deep wounds may need His loving care. Your bloody injuries might require bandages and balm. Your Guide knows exactly what to do – cry out to Him!

If this little book does anything for you, my friend, I hope it will encourage you to keep fighting the good fight.

Your journey matters. You matter.

God call's for endurance and faith in each of us (Rev 13:10).

Paddle your ducky with endurance — for many heavenly hosts and earthly enthusiasts are watching you raft the rapids of life in slo-mo, high def wonder.

We will always feel danger as we scout rapids and decide which way to tackle the obstacles. But, dear friends, life rolls forward like a river. You're safer in a boat listening to your Wise Guide than on the shore watching other people tackle the rapids. Marvelous adventures await you, along with the fear that accompanies living a life of glorious wonder.

We'll have to adjust midstream sometimes because of changes in the river. We may even look back and wish we had taken a different route.

Take heart! The best Guide and the perfect Guidebook ensure we are never lost on our journey.

Jesus will guide you. The Bible will give you the wisdom to map out your next steps.

Fellow travelers (like our *Red Ink Circle*) can encourage you. God made you for a purpose before time began and it is not only to survive by yourself, but to thrive by doing good to others. We are to sing with joy and thank God for the rocks and rapids. You can do this, in His power!

So, dear brothers and sisters,

Fight. Endure. Love. Yell, "Yahoo!"

Cry deeply when you need to.

Take a rest on the shore when you are winded. But ... stay in the boat until the journey is done.

Stay in the Boat ...

And follow Jesus. He's your guide and He'll keep you safe until you reach the shore.

In the meantime, find joy in the journey — Our God will go with you wherever you row!

Note from Victoria: Thank you to my beloved daughter Susan Davis for helping edit this section with extra care as well as your help editing this book.

DEDICATION: THE OTHER BOATS THAT SURROUND US

BETHANY KIMSEY

Often when we journey through seasons of life, we believe we are alone, solo paddling across raging seas or slow stroking across lonely waterways. In some seasons resting in quiet and calm. In others, paddling furiously when the waves assault the side of the boat, threatening to capsize our lives. In these different seasons we forget to look around and see the others with us on the journey.

But we long to remind you — you are not alone on these waters. God created us for community. He created us to encourage each other, to walk in unity, to pray, to exhort, and to minister to each other. As you spend time with Him in the Word and in prayer, He offers you the company of others as well.

The great cloud of witnesses paddles ahead of you and me, cutting a wake through the water.

They declare the goodness and faithfulness of God in all sorts of storms and riptides. Standing in declaration that faith is worth the fight, these men and women shout through the years that He who undergirds us with a faith that will not perish, also imbues us with strength to paddle through the hard currents.

We see them in the Word, and we walk with many in our own lives. These women of faith speak truth laced with grace and love. They call us forward, exhorting us to steer towards the very currents we fear. For they have experienced His hand and have proven Him faithful.

We often are blessed to stroke in unison with another, enjoying the beauty of sunrises and sunsets, marveling at who He is, discovering His truth together as we travel these waters.

These women are our pace setters at times, and sometimes they need us to set the pace. They offer the encouragement we require when suffering and pain weigh us down, and they speak the words of hope when we feel destitute.

> We *consider how to stir up one another to love and good works, not neglecting to meet together as is the habit of some, but encouraging one another and all the more as we see the Day drawing near.* (Hebrews 10:24-25)

We long to unite with the same mind, the same love that Christ has, sharing this season on similar waters. We invite you to paddle with us as we skim calm waters as well as when we steer through the rapids, for we desire to encourage you on your journey. He is worth it!

Finally, for all of us, boats follow. Filled with women embarking on a journey through waters we have seen, you and I are the ones who call them forth. We point to Jesus, we offer the direction we have learned in His Word and in prayer. We shout words of comfort and encouragement as storms rock and waves crash. We become like Epaphras who was

> *always struggling on your behalf in his prayers, that you may stand mature and fully assured in all the will of God.* (Colossians 4:12)

We embrace the calling to proclaim Jesus,

> *warning everyone and teaching everyone with all wisdom, that we may present everyone mature in Christ.* (Colossians 1:28)

For some, this book may be just that: a beginning that encourages you in your journey of faith. You may never have studied His Word looking for personal truths. We invite you to do this work. Exploring the further study verses will remind you of the consistency of His Word, and beginning to pray will tender your heart to know His love and truth.

If we could call to you from down the river, these waters of learning are richly stocked with His grace and are designed to grow your faith.

> *By grace we have been saved through faith. And this is not our own doing; it is the gift of God* (Ephesians 2:8)

Our faith has been granted to us by Him. So we stand in His Word, confident that what He has done time and again, He will do for us as well. We choose not to be those who shrink back and are destroyed by the rising waters, nor those overwhelmed by the storm clouds amassing on the shoreline. But rather we stay, believing *faith is the assurance of things hoped for, the conviction of things not seen.* (Hebrews 11:1)

Let us draw near with a true heart in full assurance of faith, with our hearts sprinkled clean from an evil conscience and our bodies washed with pure water. Let us hold fast the confession of our hope without wavering, for he who promised is faithful. Hebrews 10:22-23

WHEN THE CURRENT IS AGAINST US

SUSAN SANDERS

" And let us not grow weary of doing good ... "
(Galatians 6:9 ESV)

When I was 17, my parents divorced. They had been struggling for decades with my dad's alcoholism. My mother felt she'd done all she could, so she packed up her last few items and loaded her car.

I remember watching her drive away. I sat down and sobbed. My mom was my best friend, and I thought my world was falling apart.

Weeks before she left, Mom asked if I would come away with her to start a new life. I desperately wanted to leave with her, but God had already spoken very clearly to me that He was about to change my father's heart. Even though I knew I had to stay, I wanted to jump ship and let someone else sail that vessel home. Running away was easier.

Have we become a society that would rather jump ship than obey God and row against the waves?

I am afraid we often opt for what is easier instead of seeking God's will. We are fickle and glued to our own opinions. We throw away relationships like empty gum wrappers and leave jobs for greener grass down the street. When there is conflict or hardship, we frequently check out. We are weary in the fight.

But what if staying and fighting is what we are called to do? What if taking a lesser salary but being a light in a dark workplace is God's will? What if "winning your husband without a word" is our calling instead of leaving?

Have we missed the voice of God asking us to stay in the boat and row? Even when rowing is hard and the current is against us?

We would never have the Ten Commandments, the book of Job, or much of the New Testament if Moses, Job, and Paul had given up and walked away from their tasks. Look where we would be as Christians if these had chosen to leave their posts to walk a simpler or more convenient path.

And my father? One month later, he committed his life to Christ and became a completely different man, and God had me alongside to help disciple him in his new life. What if the miracle you seek is just on the other side of the next wave? Keep rowing!

Lord, please give us the tenacity to stay faithful to the task You have called us to finish.

FURTHER STUDY: 1 CORINTHIANS 15:58, PHILIPPIANS 3:12, 1 Peter 3:1

YOU DON'T ALWAYS HAVE TO BE STRONG

ANDREA DOZIER

> *But the Lord said, 'My grace is all you need. Only when you are weak can everything be done completely by my power.' So I will gladly boast about my weaknesses. Then Christ's power can stay in me." (2 Corinthians 12:9 ERV)*

*L*iving each day in a fallen, sinful world has an abundance of challenges. The reality is some days are good. We feel a tremendous sense of fortitude, productivity, and Christ-centeredness.

However, other days, problems barrage us even before arising out of bed! We dread starting the day. Yet, somehow, we shuffle our way through, concluding our awakened hours feeling defeated, weary, and very distant from God.

You may already be aware of this, but I will just say it anyway: *You don't always have to be strong.* Let that marinate.

I know that does not sound churchy, but it is true. It does not matter what your mental, financial, societal, or spiritual status is; trials, endless tasks, unrealistic expectations, tragedies, and overwhelming responsibilities at some point will creep into your life. When this happens, you will be more aware of your weaknesses and plentiful human inabilities more than ever. Life will spiral out of control, and you will be unable to hold it together. You will need strength, but your vat will be empty.

Good news: God will always have the strength you need. Remember this, even when things are going well, and you feel ok. But, especially remember this when things are not going so well, and you are not feeling ok.

God will always be stronger, wiser, and more capable. Truthfully, you will never be able to muster up enough strength for life's challenges alone. God has superhero power. Turn to Him. Ask for His help overcoming anything you are facing or trying to accomplish. God will provide everything you need to get through whatever comes your way.

Lord, be strong in me because I'm so weak.

～

Further Study: Isaiah 41:10; Zechariah 4:6; Ephesians 3:20-21

OUR TRUE FATHER

VALERIE DAVIS BENTON

> *I speak that which I have seen with my Father: and ye do that which ye have seen with your father ... Ye are of your father the devil, and the lusts of your father ye will do. He was a murderer from the beginning, and abode not in the truth, because there is no truth in him. When he speaketh a lie, he speaketh of his own: for he is a liar, and the father of it." (John 8:38, 44 KJV)*

Our perception of God as our heavenly Father is often based on our view and relationship with our earthly father. I never understood that more than when I stumbled upon truths about my own father.

Over 20 years ago, I was working as a journalist for our daily newspaper. While researching a story at the public library, I noticed bound past issues of the newspaper. Curiosity got the best of me. I cracked open the volume from my birth year, then searched for my birth announcement. What I discovered in black and white turned my world upside down.

A stranger's name was typed in place of my Dad's on the announcement. Needless to say, the room began spinning, and I was dramatically changed. It impacted all of my closest relationships. I started making personal decisions based on anger, pain, and betrayal, and I never looked at my Dad the same way again.

I spent about a year uncovering facts about my biological father, and keeping my findings mostly to myself. I discovered things about him that were in complete contrast to the Father, my Dad, who had raised me since I was a toddler.

I learned I was not conceived in love. My birth father had abandoned me when I was an infant. He did not care for me or the many other children he had fathered along his way. In my first conversation with him, he blamed my mother for his abandonment. But I saw through his lies. The more I learned about his true nature and the events surrounding my birth, the more I realized, *truth really does set you free*.

I also discovered that Dad courted my mother, even though she didn't love him then. While stationed with the Air Force overseas, he wrote to her that he had enough love for the three of us. She agreed to marry him, and he chose to adopt me, upon the condition that I not be told I was adopted. He wanted to spare me the pain of feeling or being treated differently. After discovering those truths about him, I saw my Dad with fresh, loving eyes.

My birth story initially came with shock and awe. Learning abruptly that my life story began with a lie sent me down my own rocky road of lies, deep pain, and regrets, until healing began. The truth about my imperfect fathers painted a picture of our perfect God, our Father, in a new light for me.

You see, God first loved us. He loved us when we didn't love Him. Even knowing our ugly backstory and that we were born in sin, He loved us anyway. He made a way through His Son Jesus to adopt us into His family with the full benefits of an heir, so that we wouldn't feel differently. And He never leaves us, nor forsakes us. When that truth sank in, I never looked at my heavenly Abba Father, translated Daddy, the same way again.

Heavenly Father, help me to see Your wonderful attributes and not be blinded to them by imperfect fathers here on earth, or by the lies of the evil one.

FURTHER STUDY: 1 JOHN 4:4-19; GALATIANS 4:1-7; PSALM 27:10

4

COMFORT

BETHANY KIMSEY

> " *Praise be to the God and Father of our Lord Jesus Christ, the Father of compassion and the God of all comfort, who comforts us in all our troubles so that we can comfort those in any trouble with the comfort we ourselves have received from God." (2 Corinthians 1:3-4 NIV)*

We are facing a season of hardship, conflict, and affliction. We can become so weary of bad news that we cry out to God, wondering why. My children are mourning the losses of senior year activities, college friends, independent living, and freedom. My younger children are unsettled, acting out, short-tempered, and quick to cry. Truthfully, I am lonely, missing community, and longing for regular rhythms again. We have had financial setbacks, plans derailed, and future commitments altered.

Scripture makes one thing very clear: my ability to comfort another directly links to the comfort I have received from God.

We comfort because He has carried us through adversity, not because we have just heard about the hardship or difficulty.

No, we console because God has faithfully walked us through, and we can point to Him for the ones caught in the struggle. We become His ambassadors, His hands and feet to offer comfort, rest, help, and truth to the ones wracked by hardship that feels overwhelming and never-ending.

So I wonder, what do I know of this comfort? I love what Spurgeon said about the beginning of this verse — by blessing God, we *"destroy distress by bringing God upon the scene."* By pivoting my hope away from circumstances and onto the only One who can hold it, distress and discouragement can be removed.

But if I resist or resent my struggle, how can I comfort another? If I redefine it so that I don't have to walk through the battle, or if I refuse the difficult road God calls me to, there is no ground for comforting another. When I run to quick fixes or hide in holes of denial, I declare that He is not my Comforter. And I am empty when faced with another who desperately needs to hear the truth of Who He is.

The spread of the Gospel is rapid and fierce when we, having walked through the fires, can testify to not being burned.

Hope is offered to the world when we can point to the waters that seemed to overwhelm us and then share the peace of God that restrained the despair so that we did not drown.

The world is desperate for comfort.

The body of believers is desperate for comfort.

Let us walk as comforters because we know and have been comforted by Him.

What comfort do you have in Him today?

Lord, help me destroy distress by bringing You into every situation.

～

FURTHER STUDY: PSALM 94:19; MATTHEW 5:4; ISAIAH 49:13

REFUGE IN THE WILDERNESS

A. T. WARI

> *God is our refuge and strength, a very present help in trouble."(Psalm 46:1 ESV)*

The events of 2020 took us all by surprise. Many were blindsided by all that the year had in store. For me, it was just one more thing that added to my shell-shock. You could say my 2020 began three years earlier. It involved a series of devastating straight-line winds, a hurricane, and the loss of three loved ones.

There were good things that happened, too, but the blows began to wear me down. I soon found myself walking through what I can only describe as a spiritual wilderness.

These years brought about many changes as I experienced events that were far beyond my control. To be clear though, the wilderness for me was never about running from God. It was about running to Him. It was a refuge, where all I could do was cling to the Holy One who is always in control and never changes.

I entered 2020 with cautious optimism and visions of a

fresh start. After all, this wasn't only a new year. It was a whole new decade. I had places to go and goals to achieve. Better days were on the horizon. I felt sure of it, but I was wrong. Within a few short months, 2020 decided to drop the other shoe and make herself at home.

It was the Lord who drew me into that wilderness refuge. He wanted to heal my wounds, but He also wanted to confront me about attitudes that needed to go. He wanted to free me of excess baggage that would weigh me down on the next leg of the journey.

The result was a necessary deconstruction of self that led to the process of miraculous reconstruction. At the time, I didn't know — couldn't know — that He was also preparing me for a strange stretch of road that the whole world was about to travel together. I couldn't see it then, but I see it now so clearly.

Don't dread the wilderness if the Lord decides to lead you there. It may seem like a lonely place at first, but He's always right there with you. If anything, His presence is all the sweeter.

Don't think of the wilderness as a spiritual time-out. See it for what it is: a spiritual boot camp involving one-on-one training with the Master. He'll use these quieter times to teach you His ways and His Word. Learn all you can.

Don't see the wilderness as the end of the road. See it as a rest-stop where you're refueled, refreshed, and recalibrated for the road ahead.

Am I out of the wilderness? I don't know, but I wouldn't trade the time I've spent there or the refuge I found. I thank God for my time with Him in quiet places.

I have no idea what the rest of this year may hold for any of us. Only God knows such things. All I know is that I'll be glad when 2020 decides to put on her shoes and move on.

Lord, let us run to you in everything. Thank you for using our wilderness experiences for good.

FURTHER STUDY: PSALM 145:18, PROVERBS 18:10, HEBREWS 6:18

6

LIVE AUTHENTICALLY

CANDACE ROBERTS

> *I will praise You because I have been remarkably and wonderfully made. Your works are wonderful, and I know this very well." (Psalm 139:14 HCSB)*

*A*s children, my siblings and I loved to pretend. We fought over who would be "Traci" with an "i" and get Ponch (from CHiPs) for a boyfriend. Often, we came home from school just to "play school." Pretending was fun.

Pretending doesn't always stop in childhood, though. As teenagers, we sometimes pretend to be like others around us. We learn to "fit in" so we can avoid the pain of standing out.

By adulthood, we have mastered the facade. We can pretend to have everything together even when we are falling apart ... to build perfect families with perfect children ... to be just fine without any help. But reality is still there to greet us when we lay in bed at night. It calls us out as frauds because we weren't made to pretend.

God didn't just haphazardly throw you to earth to figure

it all out. You are perfectly designed for your pre-planned mission.

Pretending puts us in all the wrong places at all the wrong times. It keeps us from the Promised Land of life in Christ. Only when we can be honest with ourselves, with those around us, and with the Lord can we begin to truly fulfill our earthly mission.

Every time we find something in our lives that we don't like — the way we look; the things we can't afford; the children who have problems; the marriage that is struggling; any place we feel we are failing; even sin in our hearts — we will fight the tendency to pretend.

When we choose instead to live authentically, taking these concerns honestly before the Lord and letting Him work in our hearts, we find ourselves closer to the amazing work that God intended when He created us.

Lord, help me to be real and stop pretending.

∾

FURTHER STUDY: PSALM 139, GENESIS 1:26-27, JOHN 15:16, Isaiah 41:9, Jeremiah 1:5, Galatians 1:15

7

JESUS IS THE "I AM," NOT THE "I AND"

VICTORIA RUTH DAVIS

> *Jesus told him, 'I am the way, the truth, and the life. No one comes to the Father except through me.'" (John 14:6 NLT)*

In the Old Testament, people talk about God in two major ways — "the Lord *your* God" and "the Lord *my* God."

Is the God on the pages of this devotional book the God of us writers? Or can you, the reader, say "He is *my* God?" Can you own Isaiah 12:2?

> "See, God is *my* salvation. I am confident and unafraid; For the Lord God is *my* strength and *my* song, And He has become *my* salvation." (CJB)

You can fake and lie to yourself and everybody else, but Jesus is real and if you know Jesus, **you know it**.

Jesus says "I am" which means right now. Even if Jesus was your salvation in your past, He is never a "has been" for

Christians. He is always here now. You don't have to wait for a moment to come to God.

Are you afraid and without confidence? Is it because you are looking at other "ways," other "truths" besides Christ? Jesus says He is "**the** way," not **a** way.

It isn't "Jesus *and* a political party are the way, the truth, and the life," or "Jesus *and* my family," or "Jesus *and* my country,"or "Jesus *and* my family traditions," or "Jesus *and* fall football."

If you're putting an "**and**" on your faith, that "Jesus and __*insert idol here*___ are the way, the truth, and the life,"— then you don't believe this verse at all.

This pandemic teaches me to get upon my knees each morning to worship Jesus — the only way, the only truth, and the only life I ever need.

Should I die upon my knees in the early hours of the morning, it will not be in fear of the world and the heartaches that swirl around me like a bottomless whirlpool. If I die upon my knees in prayer, it will be that my heart has burst with joy! Because no matter what I face in the day ahead, my Lord is good and in Him I am confident and unafraid!

If you do not know Jesus. Now! Do not rise until you can say, "*my* God and Savior."

If you have looked at other ways, if conflicting "truths" confuse you, if you forgot about the amazing life you can have, do not rise until you have laid aside everything but Jesus. Do not rise until you can say, "He is *my* strength and *my* song."

Lord Jesus, speak to the heart of every reader today. Let them settle that they are Yours and You are theirs alone. Jesus, you are the "I am," not the "I and."

~

FURTHER STUDY: MATTHEW 15:8; I SAMUEL 15:30; PSALM 73:25-26, John 14:6

8

REMEMBER THE PROMISE

SUSAN SANDERS

> *For all the promises of God are "Yes" in Christ." (2 Corinthians 1:20a BSB)*

I can still remember the fifth-grade boy's handwriting on the outside of the well-worn envelope. "To the One I Love." The penciled letters had faded over the two years of middle school, but I held onto the promise that John Jefferies had given me on the playground, and kept the note tucked discreetly in my school notebook, year after year.

Unfortunately, John Jefferies had become Mr. Popular after fifth grade and had walked away from the sentiment in that letter. He ignored me and was embarrassed to be associated with me. That was never more clear than the day in seventh grade when John announced loudly from the front seat of the bus that he hated me. I was crushed. My face beet red, I sat in silence. In front of all our peers, he acted as if he never promised me anything.

So, the next day on the bus ride home, I took out my tattered envelope and love letter and waited for my opportunity. As we neared my stop, I walked to the front of the bus with all the gusto I had, held up the letter, and screamed, "John Jefferies wrote me this love letter in fifth grade and promised he loved me. He is a liar!" The door opened, and I ran down the steps, holding the proof that I was right.

That day on the bus never changed anything. It was not about love; it was about knowing what I believed all those years was true and holding in my hands the proof of a promise.

We have a love letter from God — proof of His promises — but His love is not based on immature feelings that change over time. He never changes. His Word is documented truth, rock-solid promises He doesn't walk away from.

Some of us need to go back to our promise.

Remember that? Those words God spoke to us in our darkness? The ones buried under our hurt, our fear, our despair? Have we forgotten what God said or His Bible full of promises to us? Let's pull out the Word of God, refresh our memory, and renew our hope in what He has told us. He remembers all His promises and is working to fulfill each one in His time.

Lord, renew my passion for Your Word — full of promises for me.

FURTHER STUDY: JOSHUA 21:45, HEBREWS 10:23, ROMANS 4:21

9

THE LAST TO KNOW

ANDREA DOZIER

> " *Don't worry about anything; instead, pray about everything. Tell God what you need, and thank him for all he has done.*" *(Philippians 4:6 NLT)*

J thought I had it all figured out. I had managed to get through the day, barely, but I made it. Whew! Once the kids were in bed, I collapsed as usual across my bed. "My God! Why me? Andrea," I called to myself.

"Did you eat at all today? What about a shower? Have you had any adult conversations lately? Uh, I know you didn't floss, but did you at least *brush* your teeth today? Girl, you have got to do better! But you can start again in the morning because after all, His compassion is new every morning. Press reset and unplug yourself!"

Same song. Heavier and heavier each night. Nights turned into weeks. Followed by months. Then I noticed one year, two years, five years. My God, where does this get easier?

Fast forward 12 years later … My oldest son is graduating

from Marine boot camp! Watching him march in step with his other fellow recruits, I was reminded of all the things the enemy threw at me regarding my sons over those years. I read the statistics about one-parent homes. I saw the movie. I heard the clamor.

The odds were definitely against three African-American boys living on a dirt road in rural Southwest Georgia in a single-parent home with their mom.

As I stood there, holding back tears of joy, the weight of anxiety and apprehension was lifted from my person. I felt much lighter. My posture improved. My breathing became more relaxed. My capillaries and arteries vasodilated to increase circulation throughout my body.

Finally, I could exhale. I finally got it. That son belonged to God. What a relief! Someone told me they prayed for my boys and me. Someone told me that God would help me. I had read it. I had sung it. Now I *knew* that God heard and answered my pleas for help. From the first night of single momma-hood to this graduating moment. God swooped us up and preserved us.

Now I ask myself, "Andrea, others believed God on your behalf when you doubted. Others interceded for you. Repeatedly, you heard about God's faithfulness."

But now, before me was this young man in blue pants and black top, pristine-as-can-be Marine uniform. No longer was there apprehension about God's love. No longer did I wonder how it would all turn out.

Someone told me. I had read it. Now I lived it. But I guess I was the last to know.

Lord, give us people who need our prayers today and be there for them even if they are the last to know you are right there.

～

FURTHER STUDY: MATTHEW 6:28-20; I PETER 5:7; Deuteronomy 31:8

RESTING IN HIS STORY

BETHANY KIMSEY

> *The unfolding of your words gives light; it imparts understanding to the simple. I open my mouth and pant, because I long for your commandments.*
>
> *Turn to me and be gracious to me, as is your way with those who love your name. Keep steady my steps according to your promise, and let no iniquity get dominion over me." (Psalm 119:130-133 ESV)*

While reading a book to my preschoolers, I noticed a pattern with one child. This child is very inquisitive, impatient, seeking, and engaged, so every time a new page was turned, he would begin a barrage of questions about what was illustrated on the page.

I knew all the answers were within the writing on that page. I understood that nothing was unclear if he would just wait for me to read the story, yet he could not sit quietly and listen.

He was struggling to rest in the reading. He resisted

trusting the author's unfolding of the tale; instead, he wanted all the answers immediately with each new picture.

And just like that, the Holy Spirit began to speak to my heart. I often am like this child. I cannot see how all the pictures in my life fit together, the dreams, reality, people, places, talents, hopes, how they all fit in this page of my life. And I am impatient to know.

The answers are all there, written by the greatest Author who knows that my story's ending results in His glory and praise. But I resist resting within the reading.

I resist waiting for the unfolding of His story in my life — I yearn instead to know, I want to know it all, the next step, the next truth, the next way I should go.

Do you struggle here?

The psalmist reminds us that the unfolding of His word brings light to our dark places — to discouragement that threatens to cloud our perspective, to anxiety creeping at the edges of our happiness, to the doubt that threatens our peace.

While He is very faithful to reveal and lead, He does call you and me to abide in His love, dwelling with Him as He reads our pages. Our posture of waiting eagerly, longing to listen, pleases Him.

Nothing delights Him more than holding us closely and walking with us for that is where He receives glory.

The promise that He will turn and be gracious to us in the middle of our questioning, in the middle of our wondering, because we love His name should assure us.

We are welcomed and tucked into our gracious Heavenly Father's arm as He reads His story aloud for our lives.

Lord, let me have your understanding of your promises. Be gracious to me.

~

FURTHER STUDY: PSALM 131:2; PSALM 145:8; ISAIAH 30:18

SUFFERING SHAPES US INTO SUCCESSFUL SERVANTS

VICTORIA RUTH DAVIS

> **Though He was God's Son, He learned obedience through what He suffered."** (Hebrews 5:8 HCSB)

When I was in sixth grade, we elected class officers, and I desperately wanted to win. The kids called me "Icky Vicki" and taunted me. With no friends to nominate me, I nominated myself for class president and lost. VP, Secretary, Treasurer: all lost. Student government: lost.

After "election season" ended, who was the biggest loser? Me. Long before there was a show with that name.

After running for maybe 20-30 offices, kids laughed at me, and I cried over each loss.

As Mom took me for another visit to the orthodontist to tighten my painful braces, I told her I believed God was calling me to lead, but nobody would elect me to anything.

First, Mom declared, "If God has called you to lead, there's nothing anyone can do to stop Him."

Second, she asked if I had read my Bible through — I hadn't. She said to also read Dale Carnegie's *How to Win*

Friends and Influence People. "Leadership is about serving, not about selfishness," she emphasized.

In seventh grade — the story repeated itself. Dozens of losses. Again. I went to Mom heartbroken. Again, she reminded me that nobody can change God's calling. Know Him through the Bible and serve Him by serving others and meeting their needs, she said.

Although I admitted I hadn't read my Bible through yet — after I left this meeting with Mom and over the next year, I started reading my children's Living Bible. I also read *How to Win Friends and Influence People* several times.

The losing streak continued in eighth grade, totaling perhaps to 80 or 90 losses. It was pitiful, really.

During this lonely, long season, I started praying and seeking God. I asked for Him to help me be a leader, for Him to make me attractive. Although kids said, "Nobody will ever love you," I asked for God to send me a man to be my husband who would love me despite their taunts. As I prayed and read God's Word, Jesus became my best friend.

Then, my chance came during the spring of eighth grade to run for high school Student Government. I asked God how I could serve them.

While writing my speech, we took the word "I" out of my speech and focused on the needs and wants of my classmates and how I could serve them.

Finally! The students elected me to be Secretary of Student Government! Later on, God blessed me with so many answers to prayer from those times of suffering, including a wonderful husband.

From that time on, I won every election, but one. This includes many at Georgia Tech, where I led several major campus organizations. Meanwhile, every chance to serve fills me with gratitude, because I wanted it so desperately. The joy and gratitude are still there.

In that extended time of torment and tears, those tears fertilized my longing to serve, lead, and encourage other people who were struggling. Eventually, I would learn that everybody had struggles — even those putting me down.

I doubt most parents today would let their child lose 80 or 90 elections. And while we don't want our kids to suffer, we forget that the Savior suffered and learned obedience, and we must, too. My Mom pointed me to Christ and pointed me to serving others. She reminded me that the fastest way to misery in this life is selfishness and the fastest way to ministry is selflessness.

Your job as a parent isn't to prevent suffering, it is to point kids to the Savior, who will use it to shape them into His servants. He was our suffering servant, and He never wastes our tears. Not one.

Our Father is a much better parent than we are. We should steward problems and suffering. Sometimes pain gives us a platform to speak truth into the lives of others that prosperity never would.

Lord, I pray that we'll know that You use all things for good for those of us who love You — even and especially our suffering.

Further Study: Isaiah Chapter 53, Romans 8:28, Matthew 20:20-28

THE INVALUABLE GIFT OF THE HOLY SPIRIT

CANDACE ROBERTS

> *But you will receive power when the Holy Spirit has come on you, and you will be My witnesses in Jerusalem, in all Judea and Samaria, and to the ends of the earth." (Acts 1:8 HCSB)*

"Something is missing," she told me, confidentially. "I try to read my Bible and pray when I can. I go to church every Sunday. But my relationship with God is not growing."

"What is the Holy Spirit saying? Have you asked Him what is missing?," I asked her and was met with an uncomfortable blank stare.

The gift of the Holy Spirit's indwelling is imperative to our walk with the Lord. This gift, after salvation, is the most important one given us through Christ's resurrection. When we believe in Jesus, God sends His own Holy Spirit to live inside of us. He is CRUCIAL to our walk with Christ and our fruit-bearing ability. There is no connection to God without Him.

The Holy Spirit will bring Scripture to your remembrance when you need it most. He will warn you of danger or sin ahead. The Holy Spirit will guide you into all truth so that you can avoid deception. He will comfort you in trials and suffering, giving you the right perspective and outlook on the situation. The Holy Spirit gives you boldness to be Christ's representative and the power to endure the persecution that brings.

The Holy Spirit is the difference ... the beautiful and incredible gift given by God, whereby we can know that our salvation is secure.

Do you feel like something is missing in your relationship with Christ? It may be that you have marginalized the importance of the Holy Spirit.

Lord, what is missing in my life? Show me.

∽

FURTHER STUDY: ROMANS 8:2-6, ACTS 2:1-5, I JOHN 2:19-27, Matthew 12:31-33, John 14:26, Acts 2:38

13

BY HIS SPIRIT - FROM START TO FINISH

A.T. WARI

> *For it is time for judgment to begin at the household of God; and if it begins with us, what will be the outcome for those who do not obey the gospel of God?"* (*1 Peter 4:17 ESV*)

You can't read Scripture these days and not see its truth unfolding right before our very eyes. With evil all around us, our natural inclination is to rush to the spiritual battlefield. The problem is that many within the Body of Christ today are far from being battle-ready.

Count the number of "I will" statements in Ezekiel 36, and then compare them to the "you will" promises:

25 I will sprinkle clean water on you, and you will be clean; I will cleanse you from all your impurities and from all your idols.

26 I will give you a new heart and put a new spirit in you; I will remove from you your heart of stone and give you a heart of flesh.

27 And I will put my Spirit in you and move you to
follow my decrees and be careful to keep my laws.

28 Then you will live in the land I gave your
ancestors; you will be my people, and I will be your
God. (NIV)

If we agree that some level of judgment is already upon the House of the Lord, we can expect a great work of God in this hour. Idols will be removed and stony hearts will become tender. No true believer will be immune. It is preparation for the battle, and the cleansing of judgment teaches us to fight in the Lord's strength rather than our own.

These are serious and complicated times. Let's be careful about putting labels on God's people if they aren't responding in the way we think they should. Let's be merciful and quick to pray for one another as the Lord does the work of making each one of us battle-ready.

Judgment is upon us, and true believers are called to the spiritual battlefield. It is the Captain of the Host who equips and positions us. We must trust that He is more than able to accomplish His perfect will in us and through us in these unusual days.

By His Spirit, from start to finish this is how it will be until His sovereign will is done.

Lord, help be me merciful and pray for others and and pray for others as You do Your perfecting work in each one of us.

∼

FURTHER STUDY: ZECHARIAH 4:6

14

TAKING DAD AT HIS WORD

VALERIE DAVIS BENTON

Submit yourselves therefore to God. Resist the devil, and he will flee from you." (James 4:7 KJV)

Where I grew up, my parents have a 5-acre pond. There, my Dad kept an aluminum jon boat parked at the edge for fishing or rowing. I, myself, spent many hours in that boat, rowing myself to a place of solitude.

But there were precautions my Dad had stressed to us before getting into the boat.

One day, a young man visiting our house wanted to take the boat out. I warned him to first pick up the boat and look underneath for water moccasins before pushing it into the water. He scoffed at my advice. When I repeated my warning with more persuasion, only then did he take me seriously.

He lifted the boat to expose a long, black, deadly snake, which immediately slithered away into the water. The young man jumped back, his heart racing, and his complexion turned pale at how closely he came to being bitten.

I won't forget how my Father's words of wisdom kept a friend from a serious snake bite.

Whether we want to believe it, we have an unseen enemy that lurks in the dark, waiting to strike when we're not paying attention. But the Lord knows exactly where he hides, what tactics he uses, and how dirty he fights. To protect us from the Evil one, the Lord gives us precautions in His Word in Ephesians 6:10-20. We're to put on the whole armor of God so that we might be able to stand against the schemes of the devil.

If we don't stop, take our Father at His Word, and first expose the enemy to the light, he will do his worst. When we expose him to the light of God's Word, he slithers away.

Father, open my eyes to the enemy at work in my life and teach me to turn to Your Word to know how to respond accordingly.

FURTHER STUDY: 2 THESSALONIANS 2:3-12; EPHESIANS 6:10-20; Revelations 12:9-12

15

WEAK PEOPLE CAN BE USED IN WONDERFUL WAYS

VICTORIA RUTH DAVIS

*D*o you feel like you're not smart enough? That you have no power? No money? Do you feel like people look down on you? That you're not much of anything? You're in good company.

Or maybe you just feel like a weak Christian compared to other people you know.

Oh, friend, if any of these describe you — praise God! For if we look at 1 Corinthians 1:26-31, these "weaknesses" aren't disqualifications from serving God, but qualifications!

 Notice among yourselves, dear brothers, that few of you who follow Christ have big names or power or wealth.

Instead, God has deliberately chosen to use ideas the world considers foolish and of little worth in order to shame those people considered by the world as wise and great.

He has chosen a plan despised by the world, counted as nothing at all, and used it to bring down to nothing those the world considers great, so that no one anywhere can ever brag in the presence of God.

For it is from God alone that you have your life through Christ Jesus. He showed us God's plan of salvation; he was the one who made us acceptable to God; he made us pure and holy and gave himself to purchase our salvation. As it says in the Scriptures, "If anyone is going to boast, let him boast only of what the Lord has done." (1 Corinthians 1:26-31 - TLB)

God loves to use the common, weak, unimportant person for His work! He loves to use those the world and their families have cast off. If someone has told you, 'You'll never amount to anything," or "you're worthless," or "you have no common sense," or even "God will never use you," then *praise God*!

God calls us *not* because of us, but because of Him. When He uses the people who everybody looks down on, then His glory shines all the brighter!

"Let anyone who wants to boast, boast about Adonai,"
    (1 Corinthians 1:31 CJB)

You don't need talent, a high IQ, a strong body, a lot of money, or a big house. You don't need to have grown up in the church or to be a college or high school graduate. To be called by God, you need only one thing and it isn't a thing — He is a person — God. You can know Him through His Son Jesus Christ.

"No eye has seen, no ear has heard and no one's heart has imagined all the things that God has prepared for those who love Him." (1 Corinthians 2:6 from Isaiah 63:3; 52:15)

Stop imagining anything in your future and get on your knees and give your "now" to God. The only qualification to be called by God is just to give your everything to God. He'll give you everything you need to do what He calls you to do — and that can be anything!

Lord, I give you my life right now. I trust you with the future. Everything I have is yours. Carry me forward in your arms of love to do anything you will.

FURTHER STUDY: PSALM 51:17; MATTHEW 23:12; PSALM 138:6; Luke 1:52

16

THE ANONYMITY OF WOMANHOOD

VALERIE DAVIS BENTON

> *Soon afterwards, He began going around from one city and village to another, proclaiming and preaching the kingdom of God. The twelve were with Him, and also some women who had been healed of evil spirits and sicknesses: Mary who was called Magdalene, from whom seven demons had gone out, and Joanna the wife of Chuza, Herod's steward, and Susanna, and many others who were contributing to their support out of their private means." (Luke 8:1-3 NASB)*

"I would venture to guess that Anon, who wrote so many poems without signing them, was often a woman," wrote Virginia Woolf, in her book, *A Room of One's Own.*

While I don't agree with some of her life choices, I do concur with her observation. Even in God's Word, many women throughout Biblical history anonymously shared in the true story of Jesus.

Merriam-Webster defines anonymous as "of unknown

authorship or origin; not named or identified; lacking individuality, distinction, or recognizability."

It describes a vast majority of women, who have been devoted to serving God, family, church, and community, and making a difference, behind the scenes and without notoriety.

In Luke 8, we first see women noted as Christ's disciples. Their role was to minister to the male disciples who proclaimed the kingdom of God. These "certain" women, or female disciples, cooked, served, and provided from their resources to help further the kingdom.

This Scriptural text follows the account of Jesus' response (Luke 7:36-50) to a sinful woman, whose courage emboldened her to enter the home of a Pharisee, who had invited Jesus to dine with him. While the Pharisee failed to honor his guest with customary social graces, this anonymous woman wept, washed Jesus' dirty feet with her tears, then dried them with her hair. The host failed to recognize Whose presence he was in, but the unidentified woman kissed His feet and anointed them with perfume from her alabaster vial, sacrificed for this occasion to honor Jesus.

These "certain" women probably heard about how Jesus had received her kindness, praised the way she had ministered to Him, put this unappreciated woman in the limelight, and defended her when no one else had. What's more, He forgave her sins, because she had given and loved much. Her faith in Him had saved her.

You may be among many women feeling overwrought and like you're disappearing during this pandemic under mounds of thankless work.

Laundry, dirty dishes, groceries to buy and sanitize, meals to plan and cook have multiplied exponentially. Sheltering-in-place meant homeschooling, more messes, family drama, and activities needed to keep everyone occupied.

You may think no one sees you. No one appreciates what you do in the background of your family story. No one remembers your name or to say "Thank you."

The LORD was the "God who sees" to Hagar and "who heard" her child's cry in the wilderness. He transformed the orphan Hadassah into Queen Esther to help save her people. When Mary of Bethany spent her precious perfume to anoint Jesus for burial, He defended her sacrifice, saying, "She has done what she could ... wherever the gospel is preached ..., what this woman has done will also be spoken of in memory of her." (Mark 14:8-9 NASB) To the handmaid Mary, who through her humility found favor with God and was highly blessed, He was her son and Savior. He forgives all our sins if we love and honor Him daily.

You're not anonymous to Jesus, who knows your name, called you for such a time as this, and sees the work of your hands. It's His favor, recognition, love, and blessing we seek, not man's.

Thank You, Lord, for calling me as a disciple with specific purposes that serve You, Your kingdom, and others.

FURTHER STUDY: GENESIS 16 AND 21; ESTHER 4:14 AND 9:26-32

17

THE STUFF

ANDREA DOZIER

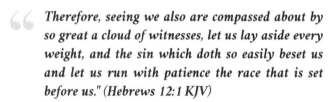

Therefore, seeing we also are compassed about by so great a cloud of witnesses, let us lay aside every weight, and the sin which doth so easily beset us and let us run with patience the race that is set before us." (Hebrews 12:1 KJV)

One day as I was in my bedroom, I began tidying it up. As I looked around, I noticed boxes, crates, shoes, and clothes. There was just a lot of stuff everywhere!

"How could I have let my bedroom become filled with so much stuff?" I asked myself.

Working from home had its benefits, but an office in your bedroom wasn't one of them!

"I could be so much more productive, if it weren't for all this stuff!" I told myself.

Then I thought about my life and all the "stuff" in it:

- The stuff of people's opinion
- The stuff of people's actions

- The stuff I told myself and only myself
- The stuff I worried about that never happened
- The stuff that I was far too embarrassed to even talk about
- The stuff I wish I had never done
- The stuff I watched on TV
- The stuff I listened to on the radio
- The stuff I viewed on social media
- The stuff that was not a big deal, but evolved into a big deal because I became obsessed with it

Self-evaluation led me to pray and begin purging of unnecessary, distracting stuff. If it was not cultivating my walk with God, it should not have precedent in my life.

I didn't have time to waste on useless stuff that weighed me down, did not count for eternity, and would not matter one or two years from now!

Anything in my life that distracted me from God needed to go!

"I am to live purposefully for The Kingdom of God!" I said.

Ok, so that was the conversation I had with myself. What about you? Do you have stuff that you need to dispose of? What's in your life that could be considered as stuff and keeps you distracted?

Are there things, thoughts, habits, or friends in your life that steer you from living on purpose for God's Kingdom?

If so, confess them to God and allow Him to remove the unnecessary stuff in your life in Jesus' name.

Lord, show me the stuff that needs to be removed from my life that is distracting me from serving you.

FURTHER STUDY: ROMANS 12:2; PSALM 51:10; JEREMIAH 29:13; Psalm 91:14

18

MIMICRY

CANDACE ROBERTS

> *For such people are false apostles, deceitful workers, masquerading as apostles of Christ. And no wonder, for Satan himself masquerades as an angel of light. It is not surprising, then, if his servants also masquerade as servants of righteousness. Their end will be what their actions deserve." (II Corinthians 11:13-15 NIV)*

Back in March of this year, my first ever mammogram turned up a lump. After several more tests, my doctors were almost certain that I had breast cancer. However, when my surgeon removed the lump so it could be more closely examined, it was found to be a benign growth that exactly mimics cancer. Praise the Lord, I was freed from one of the scariest diagnoses of my life.

In these unprecedented times, to quote anyone who starts a speech these days, there are so many thoughts and ideas swirling around us and vying for our attention. Many of these things are mimicry. Some things that seem bad are actually good, and many things that seem good are actually bad. Everything in this season requires closer examination.

We were warned that in the last days people would be deceived by mimicry. We were even told that Satan can cloak himself as an angel of light. It is dangerous for us, as believers, to think and believe haphazardly. Instead, we need to stop, examine, and research the things that we are reading, seeing, and hearing before we believe them and pass them on. We need to make sure that our loyalties to any information line up with the Truth in God's Word.

Mimicry can lead us to harmful beliefs, thought processes, conversations, and even actions. What if my doctors had treated my lump like it was cancer, based on their initial assumptions? We might have even considered a double mastectomy. Instead, we took the time to go through an examination process, to do research, and yes, we even had to do a little surgery to get to the truth.

Exposing mimicry will require us to stop and examine our hearts. It will force us to take the extra time to research the narratives we are being fed. It will make us think before believing, repeating, or sharing. Yes, sometimes Truth will require surgery, as we give up what has been a part of us for so long in exchange for actual reality, but it's only the Truth that sets us free. Don't fall for any mimicry.

Lord, examine what I'm reading, seeing and hearing and give me discernment to know what is genuine and what is mimicking the truth but is really a lie. Show me the truth, in Jesus name.

FURTHER STUDY: MATTHEW 6:23; ISAIAH 5:20; JOHN 8:31-32

19

OUR SHIELD AND BUCKLER

BETHANY KIMSEY

> *He who dwells in the shelter of the Most High will abide in the shadow of the Almighty. I will say to the Lord, 'My refuge and my fortress, my God, in whom I trust.' For he will deliver you from the snare of the fowler and from the deadly pestilence. He will cover you with his pinions, and under his wings you will find refuge; his faithfulness is a shield and buckler. You will not fear the terror of the night, nor the arrow that flies by day, nor the pestilence that stalks the darkness, nor the destruction that wastes at noonday." (Psalm 91:1-6 ESV)*

I have struggled over the last few months. Wrestling and wailing, grieving for what has changed our lives, and worrying about what will continue to change. The unknown course, coupled with the stories already experienced, has paralyzed me in many ways. I can work, teach my children, clean all the things for only so long before the shadows begin to creep across my mind. For change has come.

Yet there is always a flicker, a flutter that also catches my eye. Its movement is sometimes tiny, sometimes barely perceptible. Purpose and meaning are emerging, the motion and work of God discernible in the little places in hearts, rhythms, or outlooks. His work cannot be denied and offers Him glory.

Promises abound in this passage for you and me. God's invitation to trust in Him, to hide within His refuge, deepen when we understand how He offers protection. He will cover and give shelter. His faithfulness guards us completely.

You and I are called to trust — to hide within His refuge and fortress. We have a choice to hide. We can choose to stumble forward, desperate, and subject to whatever comes. Or we can choose to hide under His wing, protected from all storms and predators and nestled close to His heart, listening to His steady rhythm of love and grace.

His faithfulness shields us. This shield completely covers and encircles us, protecting us from attacks from any angle. Firmly entrenched in truth, surrounding us, He quiets our fears, doubts, and worry.

His faithfulness is also our buckler, a full chain armor designed to cover the body in battle. When the assaults come, his faithfulness protects and supports every area of our exposed bodies. He surrounds us completely and undergirds us.

No more stagnant weeping or frozen grief — the time for relinquishing and standing behind His shield caught up within His faithful armor is now. No more fear of the terror of night nor the arrow by day becomes the rallying cry, for we know Who protects us. The days battling an unseen enemy no longer terrorize, nor will they breed despair.

Lord, help me get buckled in, shielded, actively trusting my faithful God.

FURTHER STUDY: HEBREWS 10:23; LAMENTATIONS 3:22-23; 2 Timothy 2:13

FROM EXCAVATION TO RESUSCITATION

A. T. WARI

avid's petition in Psalm 139:23-24 is a difficult prayer to pray, but it's also one of the most liberating:

> *"Search me, O God, and know my heart! Try me and know my thoughts! And see if there be any grievous way in me, and lead me in the way everlasting." (ESV)*

Somewhere along the way, we've all buried things within ourselves. It may be pain, disappointment, secret shame, or sin. It may be so well-hidden and so deep that no one even knows it's there, but we know it's there. Over time, the weight of what we bury begins to take its toll.

The idea of yielding to the Lord's inner excavation of us is intimidating. The prospect of what He might unearth in the process is downright terrifying. This is why the earnest plea of "search me" can never be a half-hearted prayer. It must be a bold petition that reflects total trust in our Maker's ability to lead us in the way everlasting.

If your spiritual growth seems at a standstill, if peace is elusive, or your world seems upside-down, consider praying as David did. Invite the Lord to search you, and be prepared to own up to whatever He digs up. This is truly the only way forward.

The request is daunting and the process painful, but when prayed earnestly, the end-result is life-resuscitation. We're suddenly free of all that once weighed us down, and this makes us more fit than ever before to journey the way ever-lasting.

Search me, O God, and know my heart. Try me and know my thoughts! See if there is any grievous way in me. Lead me in the way everlasting.

FURTHER STUDY: 1 PETER 1:7, DEUTERONOMY 8:2, PSALM 5:8, Psalm 143:10

PERSPECTIVE MATTERS

SUSAN SANDERS

> *"... plans to give you hope and a future."* (Jeremiah 29:11 NIV)

In a poem by John Godfrey Saxe, six blind men walked up to an elephant. The first felt the side of the elephant, tough and unmoving, and declared it to be a wall. The second touched the elephant's tusk, assured it was a spear. The third blind man picked up the trunk, certain it was a snake. The fourth patted the knee of the elephant and said it was a tree. The fifth flapped the ear back and forth and knew he held a fan. The sixth man pulled upon the tail and surely felt a rope.

None of these men guessed correctly! Each one was deducing from a very small and isolated perspective on a much larger subject. Do we sometimes adopt that kind of perspective when looking at the events and trials in our lives?

Perspective matters. The Bible teaches that God's perspective is beyond us and His thoughts are higher. He has purpose for each happening in our lives — whether positive or negative. He has not distanced Himself from us, but instead orchestrates circumstances to bring about His plan for our world and our souls because He cares.

Are we struggling with a difficult situation right now? Maybe it is time to think differently and change perspectives in uncertain days.

Instead of thinking about what we are losing, think about what we are learning. When faced with a new trial, my mom would always say, "I wonder what God is going to do in my life, as I journey through this season." God is always teaching us through suffering.

Instead of "what if's," ask "how can ... ?" "What if" never brings a plausible answer with a defined path because none of us knows about tomorrow. The more we ask, the more we spiral into frustration. We forget God's purpose and heavenly viewpoint. So, what do we do? We change perspectives. "How can ... " starts us in an active direction. Try it. How can I battle fear sitting at my office desk? There is an answer for that. How can I remind myself daily that God cares about sadness? That is definable. How can I help my neighbor while I work through my loneliness? Seek His answers. Seek His Word. When we do, we soon find our perspective on adversity changes.

Father, where I have formed an unhealthy perspective about my circumstances, bring Your truth to change my thoughts.

FURTHER STUDY: JOHN 16:33, JAMES 1:2-4, ROMANS 5:3-5

22

WHAT HAPPENED WHEN WE THANKED GOD FOR A JOB LOSS

VICTORIA RUTH DAVIS

*I*magine coming home the Monday before Thanksgiving to tell your pregnant wife who is a stay-at-home Mom with your two children that your job was gone! This happened to us as a young married couple. At first, we whined and complained to God. Devastated. Wounded. Fearful of the future. This wasn't supposed to happen to us.

I know we are supposed to

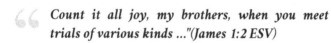

> **Count it all joy, my brothers, when you meet trials of various kinds ..."(James 1:2 ESV)**

Over six miserable weeks, God *did* provide for us in an amazing way, but we didn't count it joy like we should have.

My husband, Kip, started a fantastic job that January. He thought he was starting over. Yet, within seven years, Kip was running engineering for the whole plant. What we thought was a setback was a promotion!

As we look back, we marvel at how God provided. There

was only one problem: Our lack of faith caused us to be ashamed, along with our lack of trust and our lack of gratitude during the process as God provided for our every need. We promised each other that we would thank God if He ever trusted us with another such heartbreak.

In January 2020, He did. After receiving a raise and positive review in December, my husband came home convinced that he needed to resign due to a mis-alignment of goals with his employer. After listening to his heart, I knew he was right. He would resign and give three weeks notice. Our children weren't infants any more but we did have one in college and one going to college in the fall so it wasn't any easier.

Crying, we knelt in the office and thanked God. We thanked God for trusting Kip for the good years he had with that employer, with his upcoming sabbatical to get clear-headed, for his promotion, and for how He would provide. We believed and knew what a victorious story God would give us! We thanked God for each other, and we thanked Him for His goodness.

And we rose from our knees that day in peace.

Now, everything I'm about to tell you doesn't always happen when people thank God for adversity. But this time, it did.

For six weeks, Kip studied God's Word during a time we called his sabbatical. While Kip has always been a godly man, his relationship with God went deeper. We saw God work in miraculous ways every day. Kip overflowed with inexplicable peace and joy every single day.

Certainly his faith was tested as he applied for over 200 jobs, and only one continued to have progress. He got offers to move to other states with big promotions. But as we prayed, we believed God was saying to stay put, even though local doors seemed to slam daily.

Then, on March 13, 2020, quarantine happened due to COVID-19 for most people in South Georgia. I began leading distance learning for my school.

Yet, in divine fashion, on Monday, March 16, 2020, Kip started his new job. It was a promotion. A dream job. It was also an essential industry, so while everyone else was at home in a global pandemic, Kip worked. God had one job for Kip and closed every other door. While everyone else was going home, God showed up in a powerful way to glorify His strength and ability and Kip went to work.

Also during this time, I suddenly had two clients call me in January and tell me they had money they "had to spend with me" right then on our blog and podcast. With the urgent workload, Kip produced the podcast and met the looming deadlines. So, during his sabbatical, he drew a paycheck for the exact amount he would have received at his previous job with time left for the job hunt and to study God's Word. It truly was a sabbatical!

At the time where we could have let ourselves feel devastated and wounded, instead we saw miracles. Provision. Direction. Kip had the gift of starting a new job in the middle of a pandemic, but the miracle began with the joy and faith God gave us to greet the problem.

So, as we talk about the pandemic and the struggles we face, we want to count it all joy. The miracle is our attitude in the midst of those struggles. We thank God for problems, because they are opportunities to see God working. Jesus walks in the storm, and we can, too, as we keep our eyes on His glorious face.

Lord, let us look at every problem and praise you for the opportunity to see you at work in marvelous and miraculous ways. Let our lives be living miracles that point people to the loving and living God.

~

FURTHER STUDY : JAMES 1:5-6, MALACHI 3:10, JOHN 15, Matthew 14:22-33

23

THINGS ARE ALWAYS LOOKING UP

VALERIE DAVIS BENTON

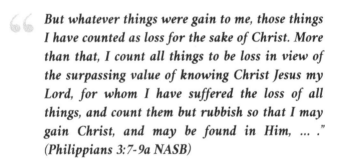

But whatever things were gain to me, those things I have counted as loss for the sake of Christ. More than that, I count all things to be loss in view of the surpassing value of knowing Christ Jesus my Lord, for whom I have suffered the loss of all things, and count them but rubbish so that I may gain Christ, and may be found in Him, ..." **(Philippians 3:7-9a NASB)**

... But this one thing I do: forgetting what lies behind, and reaching forward to what lies ahead, I press on toward the goal for the prize of the upward call of God in Christ Jesus." (Philippians 3:13b-14 NASB)

The 2020 pandemic brought about by COVID-19 has made grumblers of us all at some point. Most of us have looked back and pined for things we miss, before the widespread epidemic called for shutdowns and sheltering-in-place.

We miss dining out, hanging out in coffee shops and

bookstores, and going to church, where fellowship is complete with hugs. We miss joining family at weddings, reunions, and even funerals.

2020 conversations seldom start by being thankful for more quality time at home with family, or having more solitude to rest, read God's Word, or pray. It's rare to hear someone, during these days of uncertainty and unrest, say they are thankful for the roof under which they shelter-in-place, unmissed meals during a growing famine, or healthy family members in the midst of a global health crisis.

Focusing heavily on losses and the way things used to be turns to depression and keeps us stuck in place.

My husband is a runner. I've never heard him or other runners recount times they stopped in the middle of a race to look back at all the runners lagging behind, to trace their steps, or to review the scenery they ran past. Each runner is focused on what's ahead, who's ahead, and who is running alongside them, challenging and encouraging them on to victory.

Our journey in our eternal relationship with the Lord is like a footrace. Paul reminds us that knowing Jesus gives us reasons to move forward and to look up. Looking back at our losses pales in comparison to what is ahead for us as believers in Christ. Our focus is on Jesus, who has already won the race. He is our prize. Our eternal fellowship is with Him. There will be no social distancing, or looking back, or pining for what was where we're headed, when we place our faith in Jesus.

We press on for the prize of the upward call, or invitation, God has extended to us to know His only Son. You see, for believers, things may look grim here on earth, but when Christ is the end goal, things are always looking up. We need only to look up, and focus on Him, who is seated at the right hand of the Father. Things are always looking up, when we say "Yes!" to that invitation every day — if we're looking up!

Lord, help me to remember to keep looking up and stay focused on You.

∾

FURTHER STUDY: 1 CORINTHIANS 9:24-27; HEBREWS 12:1-2

24

'TOXIC' TO TRANSFORMED

SUSAN SANDERS

You need to persevere..." (Hebrews 10:36 NIV)

I was recently talking with a young mom struggling in the relationship with her mother-in-law. A Christian counselor had advised this young mom to walk away from the relationship because it was "toxic" and non-redeemable.

I could clearly see a pattern of the mother-in-law over-stepping some boundaries and being too outspoken in her approach regarding her grandson. However, it was also clear that the mother-in-law was not malicious but wanted to do what she felt would protect the grandchild and keep him safe.

The problem was not a "bad" mother-in-law. The problem was these two women needed to learn how to communicate their thoughts clearly, without feeling judged or misunderstood. They also needed to know when to keep silent. Both of these women loved this little boy immensely. That counselor advised this young woman to walk away from a lifetime of love and support.

I reminded this new mom that her mother-in-law would love this little boy more than just about anyone else on the planet and would be a lifelong support. It would be in this mom's best interest to invest in the mother-in-law, kindly setting clear boundaries and expectations. One day the grandmother may have far-reaching influence. She may be the one who saves for his college or shows up at every game he plays. Was terminating this relationship wise in God's eyes?

Just because we may have conflict with a family member doesn't mean we always need to walk away from the relationship. Seek God's help and clarity. Ask questions. Listen with an open heart. Be ready to invest. Just like that young mom, we may find that "toxic" person becomes one of our most devoted cheerleaders in life!

Jesus, I want to honor You in all my relationships in life, so I need wisdom to help me do that.

FURTHER STUDY: ECCLESIASTES 4:12, 1 PETER 4:8, 1 Thessalonians 3:12

2 5

THE GREAT DISCOVERY

A.T. WARI

> *Whatever you do, work heartily, as for the Lord and not for men." (Colossians 3:23 ESV)*

*I*n 1937, 16-year-old Judy Turner sat at the counter of a small Hollywood cafe. As she sipped her soda, she caught the eye of a gentleman who was instrumental in launching her wildly successful career. The girl at the soda fountain was classic-film star Lana Turner.

The story may be unfamiliar to younger generations, but the sentiment behind it is certainly not. The idea of being launched into instant stardom is almost irresistible to many in our celebrity-obsessed society. With the advent of social media, the prospect of going viral and being discovered seems more attainable than ever before.

But is the pursuit of fame, success, or popularity really what life in Christ is all about? Some believers seem to think of these things as entitlements or even indicators of a higher spirituality. The problem is that nothing in Scripture supports these views.

There are many days when what we do isn't noteworthy

in the eyes of the world. Our efforts are neither tweetable, Instagrammable, or Facebookable. Our contributions may go unnoticed, without applause, or even a simple thanks. We almost feel invisible as we go about our ordinary lives. In this popularity-driven culture, we forget that no undertaking is insignificant when done for the glory of our God.

> "Whatever you do, work heartily, as for the Lord and not for men, knowing that from the Lord you will receive the inheritance as your reward. You are serving the Lord Christ." (Colossians 3:23-24 ESV)

Fame, popularity, and success will one day pass away, but when done for the Lord, even the simplest of tasks are beautifully transformed into a reflection of His never-ending glory.

Stars will rise, and stars will fall, but the lasting reward of working for the Lord is truly a great discovery for us all.

Lord, let me rejoice that you see everything I do — big or small. Let me discover the joy in the fact that you notice everything I do. Let my work be an act of worship today.

FURTHER STUDY: ECCLESIASTES 9:10, ROMANS 14:8, EPHESIANS 6:6-7

THE TRANSITION

ANDREA DOZIER

> *He which testifieth these things saith, Surely I come quickly. Amen. Even so, come Lord Jesus."*
> *(Revelations 22:20 KJV)*

o you sometimes get tired? Life can unexpectedly take away so much, but a better day is on the horizon. That, friend, is astonishing news!

One day, the most astonishing transition will occur. Those that are weary will find eternal rest. As promised, Jesus is coming back. Everything will be made entirely right. Jesus' believers will be eternally transitioned from the barren, thirsty, and withered to the glorified, replenished, and forever fulfilled people.

What we cry about while here on earth will remain here on earth. There is no crying in heaven. We've probably all experienced some type of illness during our time on earth. I have great news! There is no sickness in heaven. Actually, things that currently devastate our earthly souls to the core and cause indescribable misery will remain on earth.

Now ponder this, what is it that seems to presently occupy your earthly mind, soul, and spirit? Is it your kids? What about your job or your marriage? How's your health? Do you wonder about the current state of our world? These concerns are quite real, but these concerns are also temporary. Don't get buried in the temporary issues here on earth and miss out on the eternal bliss in heaven. We were not made to live on this earth forever. We were created for the transition — the transition from this earth to be with Jesus forever in heaven.

Does your soul need to transfer? I know I have been talking about heaven, but heaven is only for those who have accepted Christ. I am leaving this earth, and I want you to come with me! Transfer your heart and soul from yourself over to Jesus today if you have not done so already. Time is essential! Give Jesus the remainder of your life. It is not too late. Sign up for the transition.

You have not messed up too severely. Jesus can save you.

Admit that you are a sinner (Romans 3:23). Believe that God raised Jesus from the dead (John 1:12). Confess that Jesus is Lord (Romans 10:9).

Find a church to help you with your decision to follow Christ. Hurry, do not delay. You don't want to miss this occurrence! Shortly, the skies will open, Jesus will return, and we will transition and finally go home.

For we have not here an abiding city, but we seek after the city which is to come." (Hebrews 13:14 ASV)

Lord, I admit that I'm a sinner and believe that God raised Jesus from the dead. Jesus is my Lord and I want to follow Him the rest of my life.

FURTHER STUDY: ROMANS 3; JOHN 5:24; JOHN 14:2-3

THE MUSIC HE RESTORES

BETHANY KIMSEY

> *Search me, O God, and know my heart! Try me and know my thoughts! And see if there be any grievous way in me, and lead me in the way everlasting!" (Psalm 139:23-24 ESV)*

There is therefore now no condemnation for those who are in Christ Jesus." (Romans 8:1 ESV)

*A*ll of our children are learning to play the piano. They are expected to practice every day working on scales, theory, melody, chords, and all the different parts of music that combine to make beautiful sounds that they will love to play for years. At least, that is our hope as parents!

One day as I sat down with our 4 year old to work on his pieces, he declared that the piano was broken. Sure enough, while five keys could be pushed down, they wouldn't rise again, and the sound was wrong. All the other children had practiced that day, yet no one had complained until I began to ask. Then, they all confirmed that the piano was broken, but they had just gone through the motions of playing.

I took off the piano lid and began to look around. A pile of tortilla chips was hidden on some strings, perhaps for a mid-practice snack? While I cleaned those out and rid the piano of two pencils that had also fallen within, none of these messes impacted the five keys. Confused and irritated, I finally listened to my 4 year old's words, "I put money inside. I was hiding my money." Nestled under each piano key was a quarter, wedged all the way under, impossible to grab. Tweezers extracted the hidden treasure, and the piano began to play again.

Often we can be like this piano in our walk with God. We will shove something within: want or desire, perhaps something important, something we treasure. Instead of it benefitting or simply residing there, the wedge causes massive failure to a part of my life that should make music for the King.

We may ignore it for a season, believing we don't have to use those notes. Then we begin to play the music that avoids that range, limiting our melodies. We may forget why our life's music is stunted. Until you and I seek Him again. Until we sit with our Teacher and allow Him to inspect us. As He begins to look within, He extracts what we have hidden, bringing into light the thoughts, beliefs, or longings that oppose His redemptive song.

Our hope anchors in His grace in these moments. Unsurprised by the hidden, never shocked nor worried about removing the offending items, God does not condemn us. He knows that removal is critical for our playing for His glory.

Where have you ignored stuck notes? Where are we settling for limited music because of things we have hidden or idols we have treasured?

Search our hearts, lead us instead in the way everlasting, Lord.

~

FURTHER STUDY: ROMANS 8:26; PSALM 44:21; HEBREWS 4:12

HE KNOWS HOW THE STORY ENDS

CANDACE ROBERTS

> *Your eyes saw my unformed body; all the days ordained for me were written in your book before one of them came to be."(Psalm 139:16 NIV)*

I'm becoming aware of one of the reasons why I love to write fiction.

I know how the story is going to end.

When my characters experience conflict or difficult circumstances, I'm not worried for them. I may empathize with their emotions in the scene, but I don't despair, because I know what comes next. I know the lessons they will learn. I know the rewards they will reap. I know all the ways that they will be okay in the end.

God is the ultimate story writer. When we surrender our lives to the pages He has written for us, we are guaranteed a "happily ever after" one day. Until that day comes, He's not worried … He's not fearful … He's not upset.

He knows how the story is going to end.

Keep following Jesus, my friends. He will not only make

everything okay in the end, but He will work together for good every plot twist along the way.

Lord, I surrender my life to the story you have written for me. I know you will work all things for good even if I don't understand at the time.

$\sim$

FURTHER STUDY: JEREMIAH 29:11; ISAIAH 53:4; HEBREWS 4:15

29

WHY ARE YOU ANGRY?

VALERIE DAVIS BENTON

> *"Then the LORD said to Cain, 'Why are you angry? And why has your countenance fallen? If you do well, will not your countenance be lifted up? And if you do not do well, sin is crouching at the door; and its desire is for you, but you must master it.'" (Genesis 4:6-7 NASB)*

I stare at the Lord's question to Cain: "Why are you so angry?" As I linger on this question, I feel the Lord burrowing into my heart for an answer to the same question.

No doubt, He notices my countenance, especially when I scowl more often than I smile. Whereas Cain did not respond in scripture to the question, I generally know why I'm angry.

Sadly, the COVID pandemic has also triggered an epidemic of anger on many fronts. In most cases, anger is tied to relationships, other people, or pride. I read recently that the opposite of love is not hate, but pride. And in the case with Cain, pride may have been at the root of his family squabble, since he not only directed his anger at his brother, but at his heavenly Father, too.

Are you angry? If so, why? And is your countenance giving you away?

It doesn't matter the reason why. It only matters if you're hanging onto it. Harboring anger drives distance between us and others. It sours our disposition and our relationships. It also signals to me – the individual who is angry – that I am the one in the wrong. If I remain angry, then the sin is mine, not the other person's.

Abel was not angry. God told Cain to do well and his countenance would change. Anger was crouching at the door of his heart, waiting to consume it. And it did. It hardened his heart like the ground that would no longer yield its strength and fruit to Cain. Cain missed the true harvest God wanted to produce in his character and life.

By this all men will know that you are My disciples, if
you have love for one another." (John 13:35)

We are commanded by Jesus to love one another. We are to reflect our Maker. Cain failed to mirror the qualities of the One who formed him from the dust of the ground, which he tilled for a living.

Instead, the ground became a curse to Cain as it had to his father Adam. Just as Adam was driven from the luscious garden and from God's presence, Cain was also exiled from His presence. He was cast out, a wanderer detached from most relationships – most importantly, from his relationship with God. That's the severe price of anger.

Satan's penalty was exile from heaven when he allowed pride to get the best of him. He was sent to earth, where he roams.

Your adversary, the devil, prowls around like a roaring lion, seeking someone to devour." (1 Peter 5:8)

If the opposite of pride is love, then that is our answer.

Above all, keep fervent in your love for one another, because love covers a multitude of sins." (1 Peter 4:8)

Love covers our own sin of clinging to anger. Through prayer, confession, and forgiveness for others and ourselves, we have the choice to replace anger with love.

Who knows? Had Cain put a smile on his face and let the love of God take root in his heart, he might have had a different response to God's question. And pride might not have been his downfall.

Lord, please help me to recognize when anger consumes me and is damaging my relationship with You and others.

FURTHER STUDY: EPHESIANS 4:26; 1JOHN 4:1-21

30

FIGHTING OR FLOATING

SUSAN SANDERS

> *Be strong and courageous. Do not be afraid or terrified..." Deuteronomy 31:6 (NIV)*

I stood on the riverbank and listened to the standard emergency procedures for an overturned raft. "Legs up, float on your back, and don't try to get back to the boat if you fall out. The boat will come to you." I had come to this whitewater rafting event, kicking and screaming. This "team building" trip was meant to connect us with our coworkers. I was required to participate, but nothing about extreme rafting appealed to me. I love safe. I love control. I wanted both, and this was neither.

I signed the waivers — the ones that detail how dangerous and unpredictable the waters are. I chose my paddle and climbed in, my knees shaking. Our raft guide began with introductions, but all I could think of was my fear. With a river full of Class IV and V rapids ahead, this was going to be a long three-hour trip.

As we paddled downstream in the lazy current, I heard the Lord's gentle words to me. "Susan, you can hang on to that fear the whole way down this river and grumble for the next three hours, or you can trust the guide in your boat to know what he is doing, and Me to know what I am doing." At that moment, I made a choice. I was going to trust God and enjoy the ride, rough waters or smooth.

Life is much like that rafting trip. We are on this river, whatever the circumstances. We don't get to choose our trials. God does. And, He chooses wisely, knowing what will bring Him the most glory and us the most good. We can bemoan every obstacle, fear every possible outcome, and be absolutely miserable. Or, we can look ahead of us, set our feet in tight, paddle hard, and brave the whitewater — no matter the outcome.

That whitewater trip proved to be one of the most pivotal moments of my life. I dug my paddle downward and my faith upward and loved every minute of it, fighting or floating.

We don't know what waters are ahead of us this year, but we all have a choice to make: worry and complain or trust the Guide in the boat. He can navigate us through rough waters and make us brave for the tumultuous rapids beyond the next bend.

Lord, help us to call upon Your name when we are afraid. Make us brave.

FURTHER STUDY: PSALM 145:18-19, ACTS 17:26-27, PHILIPPIANS 2:13

WHAT'S NEXT?

SUSAN SANDERS

We have all been navigating uncharted waters this last year. Maybe storms have overtaken us, and we are spiritually adrift, or at least off course. Maybe we are on the verge of jumping ship or falling overboard in the churning tank around us. Where do we go from here? What does God want us to do? We can consider four actions:

1) WE CAN ASSESS OUR RELATIONSHIP WITH GOD.

Every person reading these devotionals came to them with varied spiritual understanding. Some of us came curious, never having heard about this God of the Bible who cares so deeply for His creation. We know something and Someone is missing in our life. We want to know God, and God wants us to know Him, but we can only know God by having a relationship with His Son Jesus.

A simple, heart-felt prayer starts that lifelong friendship with God. "Jesus, I have done wrong. I have made a mess of my life. I need Your help. You are the bridge to get me back to God. Please cleanse me and forgive me, and teach me through Your Spirit to live in Your ways. Amen." The Bible is our best resource for learning about this new relationship.

2) WE CAN CHOOSE TO GLORIFY GOD IN OUR STRUGGLES.

Why were we put on this earth, anyway? The Bible says we were all created for God's glory (Isaiah 43:7). Everyone's life should point to God and point others to God. How are we doing? Are we a pleasing reflection of God, or are we living a more self-absorbed life? Glorifying God doesn't mean we are bowed at an altar in prayer all day or busy non-stop in the ministry. It means we are glorifying God in whatever we are doing at the moment and in every storm we are weathering.

One question to constantly ask is,

> Am I pleasing God right now with my thoughts, words, and actions? If not, what can I do to change? What would bringing Him glory look like here and now?"

Our obedience brings Him glory.

3) WE CAN ASK GOD TO FILL US WITH HIS HOLY SPIRIT.

Think of the Holy Spirit as a huge wind behind a sail. The more the sail is unfurled and the wind has access to the canvas, the faster the boat travels in a purposeful direction. The wind of the Holy Spirit is ALWAYS blowing.

We get to choose every day how much "sail" we extend by asking for God's help and letting His Spirit and His Word guide us.

If we want to change locations to become more spiritually healthy, we simply ask His guidance in our life and obey. Hoist up the sail!

4) WE CAN LEAN INTO FAITH.

The Bible says it is impossible to please God without faith. Trials come to teach us how to walk in faith. Expect them. Adversity is the barbell for exercising faith, and the more we work out, the stronger our faith becomes.

Once we have layered faith over and over again across multiple troubles, we have a strong foundation for trusting God even more in trials yet to come. We fear less. We anticipate His help because He is faithful. Always.

PRAYER FOR THE RED INK CIRCLE
TO THE 7 WRITERS OF THE GROUP AND FOR READERS OF THIS BOOK

VALERIE DAVIS BENTON

Father, I bring to You in prayer the seven women who make up the Red Ink Circle writing group — the circle You put together for Your purposes: to glorify You through the words You pour out through us to the hungry and thirsty in need of Your daily bread, Your Word, Your Son. And I lift up the readers who join us now on this writing journey by taking in the words You have expressly put on our hearts to write.

Father, I ask You first to sharpen their hearing to hear Your still, small voice in the midst of the storms surrounding them and above the clatter and clanging of the world's events. Mute the enemy's voice in their ear and in their thoughts. I pray Your voice would be heard and recognized above all the others and would be soothing to their troubled minds, hearts, and souls.

Please do not let us — daughters of the Most High and writers called out of the flock by You — crumble and fall prey to the enemy who desires to steal, kill, and destroy the work of our hands. Please do not allow him to rob us of our effectiveness for the kingdom or to rob You, God, of the glory You want to shine through us, so that others might see Your good works through us and glorify You in heaven. Help us, writers and readers alike, to recognize the enemy at work, using old, familiar tactics to drive us off course and cripple our walk, and cause us to cut short our race to the finish line.

Guard our emotional hearts, which deceive us and try to convince us to cease, pull back and stop investing what You have invested in us for the furtherance of Your kingdom.

Help Your saints to not only rise up as overcomers, but to believe that they are indeed overcomers, because of what Christ accomplished on the cross and Resurrection Day. Keep these women from stumbling and feeling insecure in their walk with You, when they have their security in You, Lord. Instill in them the will of Christ to do Your goodwill and be about their Father's mission.

Help each of us — writers and readers hungry for Your word — to become the good and faithful servants You desire us to be. We have miles to go yet before You call us home or return for Your bride. Please strengthen us mightily for the journey, so that we don't lose heart, don't give up, and don't give in. You tell us that if we overcome, we shall inherit all things and shall be your sons (and daughters). Undergird us, strengthen our hands and feet for the work assignments You've handed out individually. Help us focus on the prize of the high calling of Jesus Christ and understand the value and significance of that magnificent prize.

When we grow weary and weak and begin to lose heart, remind us to look up, to seek Jesus' face, and to remember that He did not give up — on the cross — nor did He give up on us, when we were not even worthy of His attention or tender focus. Give us the strength, Lord, to press on, to press in, and to press forward.

We love you and trust You as writers to go before us in

this daunting work, knowing You have a plan and a purpose for every seemingly unpolished, imperfect word we write, and that is to perfect it for Your Glory. Please take the hard, challenging, stressful, and strenuous work of our hands and minds, and transform it into something beautiful for every person who reads it. Use it all to point each reader to our Sovereign Lord and Master, our Savior, and Redeemer, Jesus. It's in His matchless name, I pray for these beautiful servants with pens in hand, ready and eager to serve You, and for those who receive the gift of our literary service. Amen.

ABOUT VALERIE DAVIS BENTON
BY CANDACE ROBERTS

Valerie Benton is the visionary of the Red Ink Circle. As a former award-winning journalist for *The Albany Herald* and retired hospital public relations manager, Valerie knew that God was calling her to continue to reach the world through her words. The Holy Spirit impressed on her heart to gather other like-minded writers "to be Literary Missionaries, shining the light of Christ in a dark world with the written word." She truly lives this message with a bright smile and a tender heart, even in the midst of adversity.

Valerie writes inspirational women's fiction, but also has non-fiction works in progress. She is the published author of "Greater Heights," a novel that follows the journey of a young, battered wife searching for answers in the midst of the 9/11 tragedy.

Valerie is wife to Harold and mother to two grown sons, mother-in-law to their beautiful wives, and grandmother to three grandsons and one granddaughter. Besides writing, she loves to teach the Word, sing, read, and watch old movies … oh, and drink all the coffee!

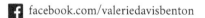 facebook.com/valeriedavisbenton

ABOUT VICTORIA RUTH DAVIS
BY CANDACE ROBERTS

Victoria Ruth Adams Davis "**Vicki**" is the brains of the Red Ink Circle. She is currently the Technology Director at Sherwood Christian Academy, but has been teaching full-time since 2002. Her award-winning blog, "Cool Cat Teacher" (www.coolcatteacher.com), and "10 Minute Teacher" podcast reach thousands of people around the world. She also blogs at www.coolcatchristian.com.

Vicki's intelligence is incredible, but it is her heart to share her knowledge that is inspiring. She is continually seeking to be a mentor to everyone the Holy Spirit puts in her path, regardless of their age, position, status, or ability to return her investment. Vicki is the published author of three non-fiction resources: "Flattening Classrooms, Engaging Minds", "Reinventing Writing", and "Do What Matters."

Vicki is wife to Kip and mother to three grown children, two dogs and one cat. Vicki loves to fish and is the inspiration behind "Stay in the Boat." Ask her about her recent white-water rafting experience.

facebook.com/coolcatteacher

twitter.com/coolcatteacher

instagram.com/coolcatteacher

youtube.com/coolcatteacher

amazon.com/Vicki-A-Davis/e/B005PBZFG8

linkedin.com/in/coolcatteacher

pinterest.com/coolcatteacher

ABOUT DR. ANDREA DOZIER

Dr. Andrea Dozier is the perseverance of the Red Ink Circle. She is a nursing professor at Albany State University and a part-time certified indoor cycling instructor at the YMCA. As a divorced mother of three young men, Andrea has experienced the struggles that life sometimes hands us, and is determined to fulfill her purpose in ministering to women in hardship. As such, she co-teaches single moms in Sunday School and also periodically facilitates single parenting and divorce care support groups. Andrea has conducted, written, and published various works in nursing education and healthcare.

Her blog, "Strength for Your Mountain Diaries" https://www.strengthforyourmountaindiaries.com/ is an endless source of exhortation and encouragement to us all.

Her sense of humor is also timely and always on point. Every now and then, Andrea finds time to read, sing, play the piano, and go outside to cycle.

 twitter.com/strengthforyou1
instagram.com/strengthforyourmountaindiaries
facebook.com/strengthforyourmountaindiaries

ABOUT BETHANY KIMSEY

Bethany Kimsey is the devotion of the Red Ink Circle. She is currently the mother and full-time teacher of eight children in all different stages of life. Bethany has a heart for motherhood and God has given her the wisdom to match it. She is continually developing resources for those of us in the chaotic trenches of raising the future generation. Her blog, "Bethany Kimsey: God's Grace in the Messy of Motherhood" (https://bethanykimsey.com/) offers the world the foundational truth and love necessary to position our children for Kingdom greatness, but also the rest and grace to refresh ourselves as mothers. Bethany has also contributed her words on websites, in devotionals, and in Bible curriculum. Most recently, she completed a Hope Writer's MasterMind and has a resource in consideration for publishing.

Bethany loves to travel, spend time with her family, cook, and entertain. Follow her on Instagram @bethanykimsey where she gives fun glimpses into her own messy motherhood.

facebook.com/bethanypkimsey
instagram.com/bethanykimsey

ABOUT CANDACE ROBERTS
BY VICTORIA RUTH DAVIS

Candace Roberts is the heart of the Red Ink Circle. She writes bravely and authentically about fear, panic, and the stresses of modern life and God's healing in her fiction works, the "Novel Series" including "Love>Fear," "Going Back Home," and "The Calling." Her compassion for others and vulnerability to admit her own fears and weaknesses instills in everyone who knows her a willingness to be more real about the challenges of life. It is no surprise that her desire is to help others heal and find the mission God has created for them.

She and her husband have five children, three who they lovingly adopted from China. She blogs at www.missionthree.org, where she encourages Christians to find their mission. She has most recently published a mental health resource for Christian counselors and teachers. "Becoming Light" the book, workbook, and challenge journal are now available on Amazon.

🅕 facebook.com/Candace-Roberts-Writer-100134988460995
🅞 instagram.com/candaceroberts_writer
🅐 amazon.com/Candace-Roberts/e/B08DHKKYWN/ref=dp_byline_cont_pop_e-books_1

ABOUT SUSAN SANDERS

Susan Sanders is the encouragement of the Red Ink Circle. She has taught the Word to women for over 25 years as a Bible study leader at Sherwood Baptist Church and is the Chaplain for Marketplace Ministries in her area. She also speaks occasionally for Christian retreats, workshops and events.

Susan is clothed in humility, and she is always busy willingly and happily meeting the needs of those around her in whatever ways that she is able. She is the author of many words in "due season." She has also written daily devotions for teachers in public and private school. She is continually searching for more ways to use her words to glorify Christ.

Susan is wife to Tom and mother to three grown children. She's raised a police officer, an artist, and her youngest is currently a college student. Susan is a lover of curling up with a cup of English breakfast tea to watch a good movie or read a good book.

Connect with Susan here: www.AlwaysDawn.com

instagram.com/alwaysdawndevotions

ABOUT A. T. WARI
BY CANDACE ROBERTS

A.T. "Anna" Wari is the wisdom of the Red Ink Circle. She is the Director of Human Resources for her family owned business. Anna is a serious student of the Word of God and has recently completed three years of Biblical Hebrew.

She is a writer and teacher of numerous women's Bible studies and loves to discuss and share Biblical Truth. Her wise words are well known in her circle of influence.

Anna is the wife of KJ and mother to two adult children, mother-in-law, and grandmother. Her passion is learning and she loves to share what she learns with others.

ABOUT THE RED INK CIRCLE

The women of the **Red Ink Circle** are seven Christian authors in Georgia who meet each month to encourage one another in their writing journey.

They seek to honor Jesus Christ in all they do. Just as iron sharpens iron, so do these women sharpen each other as they work on their craft, seek to honor God, and encourage others worldwide to find their purpose and calling in life.

This book is their first work of unified heart, crafted together during the summer and fall of 2020.